Bygone Lesmahagow
by Tom Affleck

Nethanvale Thistle, the amateur team of 1906/07 played their home games on a ground where Milton Park houses now stand. In this picture outside their pavilion is one of the Shankly brothers of the Glenbuck Cherrypickers, the most successful of whom was Bill who had an outstanding managerial career in England.

At the bowling green opening day for the summer season the custom was that the president's wife threw the first jack and to mark the occasion received a silver jack mounted atop a tripod on a plinth. The accompanying photo shows the one presented to Mrs. John Y Brown in 1930. This changed in the late 1980s, since when the lady receives a gift of money to purchase a gift of her choosing as a memento of the occasion. The Browns owned a gents outfitters in a shop where the library now is.

Lesmahagow junior football team on the steps of the Jubilee Hall, sitting proudly showing their winners cup. On their way to the final in 1885 one tie meant quite a journey: by train from Brocketsbrae Station to Glasgow Central and steamer from the Broomielaw down the Clyde to the nearest pier to the ground of their opponents. A comfortable win made up for the inconvenience of the journey.

Introduction

At one time Lesmahagow was described as three hamlets, Turfholm, Abbeygreen, New Town; collectively called Lesmahagow. Turfolm, the section on the south side of the river Nethan; Abbeygreen, Main Street and Peasehill; Newtown, south of Peasehill.

There is considerable doubt as to the origin of the village's name, but J.B. Greenshields in The Annals of the Parish of Lesmahagow gives this derivation: *The Parish of Lesmahagow probably derives its name from Les, a contraction of the Latin word Ecclesia, a church, and Mahago, a corruption of the name of Machute or Machutus, until the Reformation its patron Saint, who was born in Glamorganshire in the sixth or seventh century. Chalmers in his work on Caledonia, derives the name from Les, Lis, or Lys, British words for an enclosed place or garden; but some antiquaries doubt whether they bore that meaning. As the Saint emigrated to France and died in that country, and as in the French language Le S Machute, the contraction being written continuously, becomes Lesmachute, and means the Saint or holy Machutus, it has been ingeniously suggested that from this source the parish derives its name. The truth seems to be that none of these prefixes are entirely satisfactory; but as the second part of Mahago, Mahagw, Mahagow, is certainly derived from the Saint's name, the prefix may be dismissed as a matter for doubtful disputation.*

Early last century, except for Milton Park there were only small changes in the village, with the completion of the houses in Beechwood Crescent and additions to Broompark Drive. The 'new school' was built at Strathaven Road and was known by this name for many years until it became Milton Primary. Milton Farm moved to the outskirts of Milton Park. Milton Terrace and Milton Place were built on the site of the old farm steadings. A national scheme to demolish old unsanitary houses meant the movement of families from Gateside to an extension of Milton Park at the foot of Strathaven Road on the Creamery Brae, given the unattractive name of Creamery Terrace, so-called as the creamery lay across the road. Shortly afterward a further 'slum clearance' scheme, thankfully given the better title of relieving overcrowding, started at Woodpark and, like Creamery Terrace had more rooms to cater for the larger families of the time. Unfortunately work stopped with the outbreak of World War Two and for six years the section overlooking Craighead Park stood with only foundations finished. This was the start of the development at Bankhead which gradually extended south using up all the farm land in that area. Recent years have seen extensive building at Clannochdyke and Gateside.

The village may have been described as three hamlets, but it continued to be made up of small enclaves surrounding Lesmahagow. The old Gateside has gone completely, Dillarburn is mostly new buildings, as is Devonburn, while Brocketsbrae is still much as originally, except the railway station is only a memory. The rows of thatched cottages at New Trows are all gone and it is now a modern bungalow hamlet. Ardoch, Waterside and Hawksland, very much 'country areas', show a few new style houses, or extensions to the old, but otherwise are much the same as previously. One thing that has changed in these places, they no longer have their 'Jenny a' Things' shop.

The village was almost self supporting in the 1920s/1930s with all needs available in the Main Street from the array of six bakers, three butchers, eight fruit and sweet shops, seven drapers, four tailors, three shoe makers, nine grocers, and other specialists such as a watchmaker and a saddler. The ironmongers stocked everything from a screw nail and carpet tack to rolls of netting and roofing felt. In addition there were shops in the Trows Road, better known as the back street, Bankhouse Road, Nethanvale Terrace; at Ardoch, Waterside, Brocketsbrae, Trows catering for community needs in groceries and odds and ends. In addition to goods available through local shops the large feus at Trows, Dillarburn and other older areas show the land available at each house for home-grown produce. Many years ago only seasonal foods were used and pantry shelves laden with home-made jams and pickles. As the population became more and more mobile the villagers travelled outside Lesmahagow for their shopping with the consequence the use of local businesses disappeared which has changed village life completely. Some would say this is a sad reflection on so-called progress, while others might argue it is evolution taking another step forward. Each to his or her own thoughts.

The football match that most older supporters of Lesmahagow Juniors remember vividly is the home tie against Irvine Meadow in the Scottish Cup on 18th March 1948. The photo shows part of the large crowd in the official attendance of 16,000, but many more made their way into Craighead Park over the fence at Carlisle Road or down the railway line. Despite dominating the play the local team failed to score and the game ended 0-0. In the replay the following Saturday at Irvine Lesmahagow lost by the only goal of the game.

During the 1920s some enthusiastic golfers decided it would be advantageous to have a local golf course and arranged with the farmer at Wellburn for a piece of land where a nine hole course was laid out which served the district well for about 50 years. The photo is of opening day at Muirsland in 1935. The club finished at the end of season 1970 after the farm changed hands. By this time the local council had taken over the Holland Bush course.

Back row from left to right: Miss Smith, Miss Young, Miss Margaret Pelling, Miss Belle Scott, Miss Nicholson, Miss Jack, Miss Williamson, Miss Thornton, Miss Lizzie Pelling.

Middle row from left to right: Mr Bob Lammie, Miss Frame, Mr Lindsay, Miss McCorkindale, Mr Stirling, Miss Lindsay, Mr Bell, Miss Stewart, Mr Robertson.

Front row from left to right: Mr Cook, Miss Wardrop, Mr Livingston, Miss Fairservice, Mr Stewart, Mr Whyte, Miss McGhie, Mr Craig, ?

Almost without fail teachers acquired nicknames. There was *Low* Miss Pelling and *High* Miss Pelling, the latter teaching an older class than her sister. Miss Nicholson became *Nicky;* Miss Thornton, *Wee Poll;* Mr Stirling, *Stucky*; Mr Bell, *Ding Dong*; Mr Cook, *Auld Johnny*; Mr Stewart, *Baldy*; Mr Craig, *Ghostie* for his love of English poetry and literature with a supernatural theme; Mr Robertson, music teacher, *Tiffy Taffy*. One classic example of adapting a name to a literal translation, French teacher Miss Williamson, *Guillaume fils*. Pupils believed teachers did not know these nicknames, but they all did. On one occasion, Mr Stewart, the much respected headmaster asked the boys in a class their nicknames and said to Archie (Archibald) Garret they shared the same one, *Baldy* but for different reasons.

A display cabinet sat on the landing of the Higher Grade outside the headmaster's room and in the 1930s was filled with cups and shields won by athletic and football teams of that era. Much of the success can be attributed to enthusiastic teachers Miss Wardrop, Mr. Davy Lindsay and Mr. Alex Emond ably supported by Headmaster, Mr. Joe Graham.

Some of the football team standing beside gym teacher, Miss Wardrop's car on way to a match. *From the left*: Drew Whyte, Jimmy Hamilton, Johnie (Shonie) Weir, who was a schoolboy internationalist, and Jim Hamilton.

Joe Graham (Headmaster), Amy Irvine, Sadie Martin, Joan McGregor, Hilda Mitchell, Drew Whyte, Alex Emond (Teacher), Robert Meikle, John Reddit, John Weir, Tom Ashburn, Jean Jackson, Isobel Robertson, Jean Anderson, Isobel Martin, Minnie Turley, Helen Smith, Robert Bremner, Willie Pirrie, Billy Meikle, ?, Alex Meikle, Jack Affleck, Robert Jackson.

Davy Lindsay (Teacher), Drew Whyte, Adam Grant, Robert Meikle, John Jackson, Jimmy Hamilton, John Weir, Don Wilson, Bill Brown, Jack Affleck, Jim Hamilton, John Muir.

Across the River Nethan from the park stood the four classroom Turfholm School, its playground stretching to the fence at the river, originally the School of Industry, a girls school, while boys attended the Lower Grade at Milton. When girls were due to sit their leaving certificate they did this in the boys' school at the Lower Grade. Girls from Coalburn also came to the Lower Grade for this exam. In the mid-1890s co-education came to Lesmahagow, girls and boys started school at Turfholm then progressed to the Lower Grade. During the last war Turfholm School was occupied by a section of the army billeted in the village.

In the mid 1890s co-education came to Lesmahagow. Girls and boys started school at Turfholm, progressed to the Lower Grade School, then the Higher Grade. The picture above shows the Lower Grade School.

Mr. Matthew Glover, with an extensive knowledge of the classics was headmaster from 1879 till 1918. He was a very progressive man, his aim always being to extend the scope of education and to this end was instrumental in having the Higher Grade built at the beginning of the twentieth century. The photo shows him with a group of nine year old pupils in the mid-1890s. Two other schools served quite large communities in Hawksland and Waterside from where pupils moved to Lesmahagow after the qualifying class.

Smiddies were very busy places in years gone by and Lesmahagow had two in the village as well as at Hawksland and New Throws. A necessary requirement for farmers and carters was an almost constant supply of horses' shoes. In the photo Mr. John Dodds is fashioning a horseshoe in his Bereholm workshop. This smiddy was distinguishable by the penny farthing bicycle fixed to the roof.

With petrol and diesel driven vehicles appearing the need for the highly skilled blacksmith gradually disappeared, Bereholm being the first to close and Pathhead becoming a sorry sight before final demolition in the late 1960s. This smiddy originated as a small group of cottages known as Rotten Row. Modern houses now occupy the site.

Although the board in this posed photo says The Merry Cobblers the three older men were fully qualified boot and shoe makers, a number of whom operated in the village. As well as making footwear they did a big trade in cobbling as many repairs were done to boots and shoes before they were discarded as unfit for further use.

At the top of Jubilee Hall Brae, in the field now occupied by the extension to Broompark Drive, McRae and Haldane carried on their trade of servicing, hiring and selling the new-fangled motor cars. This area retained the name Coachwork Brae for a generation, long after the firm no longer existed. They carried quire a large staff and presumably the young lady in the photo worked in the office.

The cafe was owned by the Valerio family for many years until they moved to Lanark. The Lesmahagow cafe was then run by a series of locals but continued to be affectionately called the Tallies. Other old-established businesses included Edward McCluskie, draper and clothier in the shop facing Landykeside, later Moffats and now a dwelling house.

The man in the centre of this picture of Abbeygreen Co-op is John Clark, later manager at the Auchenheath branch. The girl is Flo McCall who lived in the strangely named Hippodrome, a block of houses in Turfholm.

The Male Voice Choir, seen here photographed in front of Netherhouse in the mid 1930s with one of their trophies, has a long association with the village having been formed in 1921. One of the originals was Tom Forrest, a member for 39 years, 23 as conductor. Before the introduction of the bus service he walked from Draffin five nights a week to attend practices. During that period the choir gained second place at Bellahouston Park in the 1938 Empire Exhibition Contest. Competing in Glasgow and the old Lanarkshire festivals, the choir became well-known and much in demand to perform concerts around the county, continuing in this vein until the present day.

This is another 1930s photo of the Male Voice Choir, taken at Craighead Park. The gentleman sitting behind the cup is Mr Cordiner of Glendevon, who in the desperate days of the depression and mass unemployment, when members could not afford to pay their membership fees, made a generous donation towards the funds.

LESMAHAGOW. I.O.G.T. BRASS BAND.
1906.

For many years early last century a band contest was held in Birkwood grounds and the village was alive with bands practising and playing in the competition. Although some band members wore suits, collars and ties, others appeared to have just come straight from work, and others such as the IOGT members looked very smart in uniform. IOGT were the initials for Independent Order of Good Templars, an organisation very strong in the villge trying to counteract the heavy drinking prevalent at the beginning of twentieth century. They had their own premises in New Trows Road next to Cordiner Church. It had a hall with a small platform downstairs and ante rooms upstairs. The Rechabites met there, catering especially for the young folks, showing lantern slides mainly on the pitfalls of the demon drink.

The Boys' Brigade Company was formed in the parish church in 1896 under the leadership of Captain Sleigh and quickly attracted a large number of boys. In later years they had a pipe band which led all the local parades, but initially they started with a flute band, their instruments evident in the 1900 photo, taken in the grounds of the old manse. Baden-Powell wrote *Scouting for Boys*, originally intending that some of the ideas could be used by the Boys' Brigade. However, boys started to form their own troops and the Scout Movement was born, the local one coming into being in 1911 led by grocer Mr. Tom McMurray. The Girl Guides followed in 1921 with meetings in Abbeygreen Church Hall. Over the years they met in various places before having their own hall built at Turfholm. They gained camping experience locally and not too far away at Crawford and Cumnock, but in later years they travelled to France, Holland, Belgium and toured part of Ireland by horse-drawn caravan.

Private John Affleck and Corporal Willie Hendry served together with the Gordon Highlanders in the Great War. Willie was promoted to sergeant and later in the war awarded the Military Medal while under heavy enemy fire for carrying a wounded comrade to the safety of his own lines. After the war he was a postman and in the early days of the 1939/45 war was one of the first in the formation of the local Defence Force (Home Guard) where he passed on his knowledge to the volunteers.

At the end of the 1914/18 war the Lesmahagow Parish Ward presented each ex-serviceman with a medal.

Lesmahagow from Carlisle Road

This view of the north end of the village shows the old railway viaduct with the Higher Grade School and Broompark Drive beyond and up towards Ellen Bank. The ground in the foreground is now Lesmahagow Juniors' football ground.

The advent of North Sea gas saw the end of the local gasworks, and the demand for better accommodation and improved sanitary conditions meant the end of the houses in the small square next to the church. With the need for the local sawmill declining over the years following the last war it closed along with its various outbuildings bordering the gasworks, so another bit of our history disappeared. The ground is incorporated in the park now.

Lesmahagow

22 March '06

KSS

An early 20th century view shows how much the old village has changed. In the background Viewbank is prominent and the third semi-detached house on the west side Beechwood Crescent not built. Centre has The Mound, Cordiner Church and housing on New Trows Road all gone and the large garden behind the bank, site now occupied by a nursing home.

LESMAHAGOW FROM THE WOOD. A.6079.

In the foreground is the top part of the bridge over the railway and reveals it to be prior to the erection of the *ambush* at the Glebe Cinema, an adjunct to the building allowing patrons to queue under cover while waiting to enter for the next showing. The view also includes Woodview, The Mound, Cordiner Church and several other buildings long since demolished.

The local railway staff had a strong ambulance team but whether or not this is their group is not known. Dr. Martin, until he retired and left Lesmahagow, conducted an ambulance class in the station waiting room every Sunday evening throughout the winter for many years, primarily for railway staff, but others with an interest in first aid also attended.

Dr. Douglas of Auchlochan, local M.P. was chairman of the Council of Agriculture which was responsible for setting up Womens' Rural Institutes in 1919 and shortly afterwards an institute started in Lesmahagow with his wife Mrs. Anne Douglas as the president. She took a great interest in the various Rurals in the district and members met regularly at Auchlochan. The photo of 12th June 1951 was one such occasion. Mrs. Douglas is third from left in second front row.

The halls were requisitioned during the war and occupied by the army. When the army left and blackout restrictions lifted the British Legion organised a dance in the Jubilee Hall in March 1945 when the hall was packed with best suits and dresses given an airing for the first big event in six years. Among the revellers was a sprinkling of servicemen on leave. Everybody enjoyed the occasion knowing that the war in Europe was nearly over.

The Jubilee, Masonic and Trows halls were in constant demand, especially at weekends and any organisation wanting a Friday night had to book well in advance. Before the Second World War, dances often lasted until four in the morning. In later years they ended at a more respectable time - 2 a.m. Trows had their annual party and the 1930 photo shows the large number who attended this function.

Several locally owned buses operated from the village. Best known was Hammy Jackson and from his garage at Auchenheath ran a regular service between Lesmahagow and Lanark as well as another to Rigside. However, his buses like those of Dodds and Love were in great demand for organisations outings to the Borders, the Trossachs, St Andrews and other popular spots and theatre visits.

From the early 1900s Freddy Palmer presented picture shows, originally in a tent where the masonic hall now stands, replaced by a wooden structure in 1920 halfway up the old Brae, always going by the name of Freddies or Palmers pictures until the modern Ritz replaced it in 1938. It went on fire a few months later and remained closed till reconstructed and reopened in September 1943. Fire again struck in 1957, but there was no extensive damage and it started up once more a few months later. Attendances were declining in cinemas and the Ritz was no exception. After a short time as a bingo hall it closed, finally falling to the demolisher in 1982. The other cinema, The Glebe in Landykeside, had already shown its last film, and Lesmahagow had no picture house after 70 years of cinema going.

These were busy days for housewives. They rose early to get a good fire going under the boiler in the washhouse ready for the first graith. The fact there were few accidents of scalding as the clothes were moved from sink or wringer or mangle was all due to the expertise of the housewife. With the clothes ready to hang outside her wish was for a dry day with a bit of wind and a good drooth when the clothes were out on the rope. The whites would be laid out on the green to bleach and if the rain came on there was a rush to lift them, for not only would they get wet, but the rain brought down soot from the smokey chimneys and needed further attention in the washhouse. If they got soaked with the rain it meant everything had to hang on the pulley inside till dry. One consolation, with the communal bleaching green there was always time among neighbours to catch up with the latest news.

When the Kilnhall Burn flooded in 1927 the debris brought down choked the culvert which carried the water under the road from Rookwood and into the Nethan at the swing park, resulting in serious flooding of Main Street and the adjoining shops. The first area affected was the Coalburn & District Co-operative and the adjoining dwellings, where Hope Hall and the post office are now situated. Cleaning up started with the council attending to the road, and shopkeepers and householders looking to their own properties. The burn was redirected to enter the Nethan across from the bowling green.

The park in all its splendour with three tennis courts, now an all weather football pitch, the putting green designed with several hazards making it a challenge to play. At the corner of the putting green stands the rather attractive pavilion ruled over with a rod of iron by a series of park attendants.

1937 was a year of celebration throughout the country and Lesmahagow was no exception. It was the Coronation of George V1 who had come to the throne after the abdication of his brother, Edward the year previously. For the schoolchildren it was especially good for although attending school there were no lessons, only a gathering in the playground to receive a small oblong tin box with a commemorative medal, a small photo and, special treat, a bar of chocolate. After a drink of milk it was off in a long crocodile line for a visit to the pictures. In the park a crowd gathered to watch the planting of a Coronation tree by Mr. John Dodds, the oldest inhabitant, assisted by Headmaster, Mr. Joe Graham, and watched by Councillor Mr. Kerr Simpson.

ABBEYGREEN U.F. CHURCH AND MANSE LESMAHAGOW

After the Disruption in the Scottish churches in 1843 the United Free Church was set up and the local U.F. church was built with accompanying manse, the new church opening in 1844. The status of Free Church remained until it became Abbeygreen Parish Church in 1929.

When the weather vane from the steeple of the Old Parish Church was taken down to allow repairs to carry on, three year old Allan Silver took the opportunity to be photographed alongside it. Allan probably pays more attention to wind speed and direction now as he is in the Royal Air Force training as an air traffic controller.

Kerse House, Lesmahagow.

Kerse was one of the estates with a large spread of tomato houses and extensive fields of soft fruit. In addition to full-time workers many casuals were employed including school children and housewives earning some welcome extra money during the fruit-picking season. A loud horn warned workers of starting time, dinner break and finishing time. It could be heard over a wide area and in the days before everyone owned a watch was a guide to all and sundry. Kerse House was the home of J. B. Greenshields who wrote the Annals of the Parish of Lesmahagow in the mid twentieth century.

Auchtyfardle stood in a commanding position in many acres of pasture land and meadow overlooking the village. It boasted two carriageways, one off Dillarburn Road and another at Kerse Road end, this avenue led down to the walled garden and the Nethan where it was crossed by a rustic bridge, on to a footpath by the river and past a tennis court. During the First World War it housed wounded soldiers and medical staff.

Two large chestnut trees grew on the lawn outside the house and when autumn arrived a notice went round the school telling the children if they went on a particular day there would be chestnuts lying on the ground. After school a large contingent of childen, mostly boys, made their way to Auchtyfardle to collect the harvest of fallen nuts, much of it knocked to the ground by the staff earlier in the day.

Milton Park housing scheme was built in the 1920s and many families moved from old parts of the village, with single ends or room and scullery and outside lavatory and washhouse to houses with hot and cold running water, bathroom, and inside wash boiler. Total luxury! There was a mixture of two, three and four room houses and those with two rooms stuck to the old Scottish custom of a set-in bed in the kitchen, as the living room was then called. Originally local authority housing they are now mostly privately owned. A small shop stood at the foot of Nethanvale for many years.

Several accidents at the Toll Corner, some serious, prompted plans being prepared in the 1930s for improvements to the road which meant demolishing the old Rescue Station houses. The tenants were relocated to Manse View, a short distance up the road. Like so many plans, changes were made and building of a dual carriageway with a new bridge over the Nethan started and work went ahead only to be suspended when war broke out in 1939, not to restart until hostilities ended. The widening of the road called for demolishing Manse View houses and the tenants who had moved there some years previously were moved again to the new houses built at Bankhead

The right of way from the village to Brocketsbrae started with a footbridge across the Nethan at the old cemetery and another footbridge was built over the railway line when it opened and stayed in place until the trains stopped running to Coalburn. Immediately below the bridge two German field guns, trophies of the Great War were positioned there by ex-servicemen and provided an adventure play area for a generation of children. During the Second War the soldiers stationed in the village maneuvered the guns down the embankment into the Nethan and hauled them to a suitable place where they were manhandled out to be loaded to lorry and taken away to help the war effort scrap metal drive.

This 1950s photo shows the railway and viaduct, Milton Cottages, Craighead tomato houses, mill store, the corner of Craighead Park and the old smiddy sitting at the side of what was the original main road connecting north and south of the country.

THE BOOTHY, MONKSTABLE WALK, LESMAHAGOW.

A favourite walk of many years ago, better known as round by the Gairden Dyke, as part of it was bordered by the wall of Birkwood's garden. Having passed there, came the bothy on the left and the dooking hole known as the Mochrie, a busy place on a warm summer day, then on over the wooden bridge spanning the Nethan. This bridge was destroyed when a tree crashed on to it during a storm and replaced by a much less attractive metal and concrete bridge.

BIRKWOOD GLEN, LESMAHAGOW. E.

A lady who lived in the house shown on page 45 cannot recall any gathering other than the cattle show and pipe band contest being held in this field, which was across a carriageway from her house, but the event may have been a gala day for children.

This is a cup with a history of vanishing and turning up again. It was gifted to the Horticultural Society in 1926 and in 1934 Walter Johnstone of Kirkmuirhill won it. That was the last flower show as the society folded due to lack of support. A new society came into being in 1961. Mr. Johnstone had looked after the cup for all these years and gave it to the new committee. This society stopped functioning in 1975 and the last winner, C.W. Dobie left the cup with the president and it lay in his house until recently, when he passed it on to the son of the donor.

A diamond wedding has always been an excuse for a family reunion and this celebration in 1911 at Nether House of Greystone George Bryson and Janet Meikle's 60 years of marriage was no exception.